Why Should I Join a Church?

Crucial Questions booklets provide a quick introduction to definitive Christian truths. This expanding collection includes titles such as:

Who Is Jesus?

Can I Trust the Bible?

Does Prayer Change Things?

Can I Know God's Will?

How Should I Live in This World?

What Does It Mean to Be Born Again?

Can I Be Sure I'm Saved?

What Is Faith?

What Can I Do with My Guilt?

What Is the Trinity?

TO BROWSE THE REST OF THE SERIES,
PLEASE VISIT: **REFORMATIONTRUST.COM/CQ**

CQ

Why Should I Join a Church?

R.C. SPROUL

Reformation Trust   A DIVISION OF LIGONIER MINISTRIES, ORLANDO, FL

Why Should I Join a Church?
© 2019 by R.C. Sproul

Published by Reformation Trust Publishing
a division of Ligonier Ministries
421 Ligonier Court, Sanford, FL 32771
Ligonier.org   ReformationTrust.com

Printed in China
RR Donnelley
0000819
First edition

ISBN 978-1-64289-207-9 (Paperback)
ISBN 978-1-64289-208-6 (ePub)
ISBN 978-1-64289-209-3 (Kindle)

Cover design: Ligonier Creative
Interior typeset: Katherine Lloyd, The DESK

Scripture quotations are from the ESV® Bible (The Holy Bible, English Standard Version®), copyright © 2001 by Crossway, a publishing ministry of Good News Publishers. Used by permission. All rights reserved.

Library of Congress Cataloging-in-Publication Data

Names: Sproul, R.C. (Robert Charles), 1939-2017, author.
Title: Why should I join a church? / R.C. Sproul.
Description: Orlando, FL : Reformation Trust Publishing, a division of
  Ligonier Ministries, [2019] | Includes bibliographical references and index.
Identifiers: LCCN 2019017410 (print) | LCCN 2019019983 (ebook) | ISBN
  9781642892086 (EPub) | ISBN 9781642892093 (Kindle) | ISBN 9781642892079
  (pbk. : alk. paper)
Subjects: LCSH: Church membership. | Church attendance. | Church.
Classification: LCC BV820 (ebook) | LCC BV820 .S67 2019 (print) | DDC
  262--dc23
LC record available at https://lccn.loc.gov/2019017410

Contents

Chapter One

Sanctified People, Sanctified Space

On a trip to the Holy Land, I visited one of the most important tourist sites in Jerusalem: the Dome of the Rock. This monument is one of the holiest Islamic shrines in the world. I was intrigued that as we approached the entrance, our guide spent five to ten minutes carefully instructing us on the proper protocol for entering into this sacred place. For example, we could not escort our wives by holding on to their arms because that gesture is deemed inappropriate for such a holy place. And, of course, we had to take our shoes off before entering.

Isn't it interesting that religions of all sorts, all over the world, have their sacred sites, their holy places? Christians often think of the church as a building, a structure, a place where people gather for worship and religious activities. For that reason (among others), many people think they can do without the church. "I don't have to gather with other people in order to be a Christian," they think. "I can worship right where I am. I don't need the church."

In our culture and in our nation, many people express disenchantment with the institutional church, and many people feel that the church has let them down and has not met their expectations. We don't often find people excitedly saying, "Oh, how I love the church!" There is a disconnect here, because we know with certainty from Scripture that Christ loves the church. And if we are of Christ, we can't possibly fail to love, or even despise, what is so loved by Him.

What I hope to do in this book is offer an apologetic or a defense of the church. I want to define what the church is, to explain what the church is made up of, and to explore the church's vocation and mission. In this way, I hope to lay out how vital it is for Christians to be joined to a body of believers.

We can quickly discover through our study of Scripture that the church is not a building—it is people. Yet even in the Scriptures, particularly in the Old Testament, the place of worship was very important to the religion of Israel. If you recall, the tabernacle was built according to the detailed provisions and commandments of God. The articles that were placed in that structure were crafted by men who were uniquely endowed by the Holy Spirit to perform their tasks. And the garments of the priesthood of Aaron were intricately designed by God's command. The same kind of detailed consideration was articulated by God for the building of the temple.

So if the church is not a building, why should buildings mean anything to us? It seems we've lost much of the mystique of former ages regarding church buildings. Church architecture has changed. Rarely do we see a new church building constructed in the Gothic style with vaulted ceilings and flying buttresses. A lofty sense of transcendence used to be communicated by the very building itself. Most of our church buildings today are designed in a more functional way. They're built to facilitate fellowship. In many cases, they hardly differ from civic meetinghouses. Yet if you go down the main street of any city in the United States of America and you come upon a church, you will be able to recognize it immediately; there's something different about the building. Human beings in cultures and nations all over the world—wherever people are religious, whatever religion they practice—find a way to establish sacred buildings.

Anthropologists say that the heart of every human being contains an insatiable hunger to make contact with the holy. All religions in all cultures around the world have their individual examples of *hierophanies*. A *hierophany* is an outward, visible manifestation of the sacred. We want to see a distinction between the secular and the sacred, between the profane and the holy, even in our buildings.

Theologian Mircea Eliade observed that the front door of every church in America has a symbolic significance for people; it is a threshold, a line of demarcation. As we step over that threshold, we leave behind the secular and the profane, and we enter the presence of the holy, of the sacred, of the transcendent.

Now, we have to be careful, because we remember Jesus' teaching to the woman of Samaria. She wanted to engage

(Church is People) ✓

Jesus in a theological dispute about the proper place of worshiping God. "Is God to be found on this mountain?" she asked, pointing to Gerizim, "or is He residing in Jerusalem?" (see John 4:20). Jesus had to free this woman of her narrow conception of the localization of God. He had to teach her that God is not contained in buildings made by hands, that God cannot be captured within defined boundaries, and that God's presence is as much in the secular realm as it is in what we call the sacred realm. But in spite of Jesus' warning, we cannot ignore how basic it is to our humanity that we desire to set apart certain times and places for special significance and for holiness.

But again, the church isn't a building; the church is people. The word for *church* in the Bible comes from the Greek word *ekklēsia*. The prefix *ek-* or *ex-* means "out of" or "from." The root of *ekklēsia* comes from the Greek word *kaleō*, which means "to call." So the church is something or someone who is called out of something else. The *ekklēsia* consists of those who have been called by God out of the world. The church consists of those to whom God has given a divine summons, a sacred calling by which He has commanded them to cross the threshold into the area of the holy.

In the Old Testament, when God summoned the Israelites to gather for corporate worship, a shofar (ram's horn) was blown. That signaled the people to leave their daily tasks and assemble in the presence of God. Often, that solemn assembly would be initiated by a prophetic summons: "Hear, O Israel. Listen, for the Lord your God is present in your midst, and He is about to speak." Even in today's church service, we begin with a summons, a call to worship, because the church is an institution that is called to worship. It is an institution *ek kaleō*, called out of the world, and its members are those whom God has called for a vocation—to be His people and to be holy even as He is holy.

One of the most important images of the church in the Bible is that of the bride of Christ. The image is deeply rooted in the Old Testament, wherein God takes a people to Himself and makes a vow. He enters into a solemn covenant with Israel. He pledges His everlasting faithfulness to His people, and in response, the people enter into an agreement with Him and recite their vows. And so a contractual union is effected in Israel. This image of marriage is found throughout the Old Testament; God is betrothed to Israel, and when Israel is unfaithful to God, the sin of her disobedience is presented in the language of harlotry and adultery.

In the New Testament, we find a whole new dimension to this bride imagery. In order to grasp the fullness of this metaphor, we must first understand something about marriage in the Old Testament. After reading the Ten Commandments in Exodus 20, we get a broader exposition of the law in Exodus 21 called "the Holiness Code." Chapter 21 begins with teaching that sounds foreign to our culture. We read about the laws and the rules governing the handling of indentured servants or slaves. One such law states that if a man enters into slavery or has been purchased, he must, after six years, be freed when the sabbatical year comes. If the man brought his wife with him into servitude, then when he is freed, she must be freed as well. But if the man was single when he entered his period of slavery, and his master provided a wife for him, and the wife bears children to the slave, then at the sabbatical year, the slave is freed but his wife and the children stay with the master. When we read that, we stumble, not only because of the whole concept of indentured servitude, but because it seems cruel that the master keeps the wife and children.

But we must understand that in Israel, when a man wanted to marry a woman, he had to pay what was called the bride-price. He had to pay a substantive fee, and that fee demonstrated that he had the means to take care of his bride and whatever offspring they would produce. The father would not grant the hand of his daughter until the bride-price was paid. Now in the case of Hebrew servants, the Hebrew master had the responsibility to see that the bride and the children were taken care of. Remember that, in indentured servitude, the husband became indentured in the first place because he couldn't pay his debts. He had no money, so he had to work off his debts. He certainly wouldn't have the money to take care of a wife and children in the event of his liberation, so the law of God required that the master would still be responsible for caring for the wife and the children until the time that the husband could get back on his feet and pay the bride-price.

Why is this important for us? The primary reason the church is called the bride of Christ is because *Jesus purchased His bride.* He paid the ultimate bride-price, with nothing less than His own blood. Not only that, but this bride whom He purchased was not pure. In the Old Testament, if a woman pretended she was a virgin at marriage and it

8

was discovered that she was not, severe penalties were meted out. But our Lord bought a bride who was not pure. He died for that bride. And He has promised the Father that He will present His bride at His final wedding feast in heaven without spot and wrinkle because He loves His bride. Christ loves the church and purchased it by His death.

deep reasoning Theology.

Chapter Two

The Body
of Christ

The New Testament often speaks of the church as "the body of Christ." The concept of the church as the body of Christ is, on the one hand, quite simple. But as we probe its significance, we discover it is also profound. To understand the concept of the church as a body, it's helpful to understand the church as a mother. Cyprian of Carthage said, "He can no longer have God for his Father, who has not the church for his mother." There have been a host of controversies throughout church history about what Cyprian meant. But I want to focus on the core of what he said.

We could say that just as it is necessary for us to have a human mother to be born into the human family, so we cannot be born into the kingdom of God unless the church gives us birth. But that's not the way we should understand Cyprian's statement. The church is not the institution that saves us; Christ is the One who redeems us, and it's the Holy Spirit who regenerates our hearts unto newness of life. Of course, the church acts as a midwife in many cases with the proclamation of the gospel, the administration of the sacraments, and so on.

But another crucial function of a mother in this world is to nurture. The mother not only bears the child but also nourishes and nurtures the child. In our culture, traditionally, the mother cares for and nurtures; the father disciplines. When we consider this image of the church as a mother, we see the nurturing ministry of the church to its members. Just as an infant desperately needs the nourishment provided by its mother, so we, as infants in the kingdom of God, desperately require the means of grace, which are focused and concentrated in the church. That is how the church acts as a mother to us.

When we turn again to the concept of the church as the body of Christ, we might think of the ways that people resist this idea. I've heard countless people say: "Look, I'm a Christian. I'm a religious person, but I am not a member of any institutional church; I don't need to be a member of an institutional church. I worship privately; my religion is personal and private. I don't need to go to church to have a personal relationship with God." Have you heard that? Maybe you've even said it. If you say that, then it is possible that you are a Christian, but it's not very likely. Why? Because when we look at the New Testament, even a cursory reading tells us that when Christ redeems an individual, He never leaves that individual in isolation.

Redemption is not a group activity. In the end, when we stand before almighty God, we will stand alone; our brothers, sisters, mother, father, friends, club, nation, or church will not avail us when we stand before God. God will deal with us as individuals, and it's as individuals that we enter the kingdom of God. But we can't confuse that reality with individualism. When Jesus redeems an individual, He places him into a group, and He calls that group His own body.

How in the world can a person love Christ and hate His

body? How can a person embrace Christ for any period of time and continually absent himself from fellowship with the company of God's people, the family of God? That's another image in the Bible: the *laos Theos*, the people or family of God. After babies are born, if they are simply set on a table in the delivery room and given no nourishment, they will die. Yet nourishment is not enough; studies indicate that if they are given food and water but no human companionship, no fellowship, they will perish.

I remember a minister who talked about how much he enjoyed cookouts. He prepared the charcoal grill by stacking the charcoal in a neat pile. He sprinkled lighter fluid over the heap of charcoal and ignited it with a match. He waited until those coals began to glow and then became white as ashes started to appear. If he blew on the coals, he could see them glow red, indicating the intense heat that the coals were generating. That's when he knew it was time to put the meat on the grill. At this point, the minister said: "What would happen if I took one piece of charcoal and removed it from the heap and set it aside? In no time at all, all the heat in that coal would dissipate. It would lose its warmth. It would become cold and useless for its task." That's what happens to people who isolate themselves from

We (Christian — hot or cold)
neither

the body of Christ and who seek to live the Christian life as loners. It is not the way God intended His people to live.

For those who find it unpleasant to think of the church as an organization, you can think of it instead as an organism. An organism is something that is alive. It's vital, it can move, it's exciting, and it's not inert or lifeless or inanimate. When we talk about that body, we're talking not about a corpse but a living thing. People want to be part of a group that's alive and vital.

The Apostle Paul discusses the body of Christ in his first letter to the Corinthians:

> For just as the body is one and has many members, and all the members of the body, though many, are one body, so it is with Christ. For in one Spirit we were all baptized into one body. . . .
>
> For the body does not consist of one member but of many. If the foot should say, "Because I am not a hand, I do not belong to the body," that would not make it any less a part of the body. And if the ear should say, "Because I am not an eye, I do not belong to the body," that would not make it any less a part of the body. If the whole body were an

eye, where would be the sense of hearing? (1 Cor. 12:12–17)

You could see perfectly if all you were was an intricately designed, magnificently constructed eye, but you would be no good for anything else. No one could have a relationship with you. We value our eyes, and likewise our ears are important to us. But the eye can't say to the ear, "I don't need you." The ear can't say to the eye, "I don't need you." The eye can't say, "I'm not a part of the body."

What's the point? Paul says the church is like a human body. It is an organism. The one absolutely necessary condition for an organism to remain alive is that it stay organized. If you find an organism that is disorganized, then you have found an organism that is dying. Paul here is talking about the church as an organized body. He's talking not in abstract categories of organization but about how the individual parts fit together to make the whole and how each part in that organism has its vital contribution to make. The body is not whole without eyes; it's not whole without ears or without hands. God has made the body gloriously fit together: "God has so composed the body, giving greater honor to the part that lacked it, that there may be no division in the body, but that the members may have the same care for one another. If one member suffers, all suffer together; if one member is honored, all rejoice together" (vv. 24–26).

This is a magnificent model. Have you ever seen someone honored in the church? Has anyone been honored in your work environment or in your school? When you saw someone else honored, did you feel a pang of envy or jealousy? If the body is working well and working together, when one member suffers, everyone suffers; when one part is honored, everyone rejoices. The individual parts never lose their individuality or their distinctive characteristics. We don't submerge our personality into an organization when we join the church. We retain our individuality, but that individuality makes its own contribution to the whole. The honor accorded to one part does not detract from the honor due to another part. We all need each other.

The people in the Corinthian community were fussing and fighting about whose gifts were most important. Factions arose based on pride. "I'm an eye; I can see." "I'm a mouth; I can talk." "I'm an ear; I can hear." But Paul says, What good is the hearing if you can't speak? What good is the speaking if you can't see? Paul says that the same

Spirit who redeemed us pours out His gifts on every member in the body of Christ. Every person has a supernatural endowment from God as a part of the body of Christ, and the body, to be healthy, needs all our gifts, whatever they are. For the body to be complete, it needs each of us.

Martin Luther spoke in the sixteenth century about the "priesthood of all believers." This concept means that the priestly ministry of Christ is not given exclusively to the clergy, as the Roman Catholic Church has taught; rather, it is given to every person in the church so that they can all play their part. We are all responsible for the ministry of the body of Christ. We have a tendency, because of our human pride, to exalt our own gifts. I might be tempted to think that if you're really spiritual, you will seek the gift of teaching. I might be tempted to think that the most important thing that takes place in the church is the teaching of sound doctrine, because without sound doctrine, there will never be good evangelism. I might make the case that if you're really spiritual, you'll be interested in theology. Now what would motivate me to say that? Because that's what *I* do, and I like to think I'm exercising the most important gift. But that's not the way it works. I should be doing everything in my power as a theologian

Preaching in church

to assist and support the work of evangelism, the work of ministering to the poor, the work of administration, and so on. We are all part of the body of Christ, we all have gifts, and we all have a part to play in promoting the health and growth of the body.

Chapter Three

One, Holy, Catholic, and Apostolic

A s we continue to explore the nature and character of the church and what it means for us to be joined to it, let's reach into the pages of church history—all the way back to the fourth century, when the Nicene Creed was composed. Many churches use the Nicene Creed regularly in their liturgy. This magnificent creed, written in 325 and amended in 381, affirms the deity of Christ—that He is God of God and Light of Light, that He is begotten and not made, and that for us men and for our salvation He came down from heaven. In addition to its marvelous teaching on the person and work of Christ, the Nicene Creed gave us a famous list of adjectives that the church has used to confess its concept of itself. In this chapter we will explore each of these adjectives: *one*, *holy*, *catholic*, and *Apostolic*.

The Church Is One

The Nicene Creed tells us that the church is *one*. In our world today, it can be hard to see the unity of the church, but when the Nicene Creed was written, the unity that the church enjoyed was indeed an organizational unity. For the most part, there was but one visible Christian church. This was before the Great Schism and the Protestant Reformation, when the visible unity of the body of Christ was broken. In the United States, for example, there are hundreds, and perhaps thousands, of Protestant denominations, associations, and traditions. We can no longer say with the confidence of the fourth-century church fathers that the church is numerically one in the visible sense, but there still is a sense in which some unity of the body of Christ has been preserved.

For example, despite the points of doctrine on which we disagree and by which our distinctives are determined, there is still a universal (or *catholic*) faith that all true churches embrace, which is summarized in the early creeds such as the Nicene Creed and the Definition of Chalcedon (written in 451). There is a common core of truth that every true church affirms. We all believe in the Trinity. We all believe in the deity of Christ. We all believe in the work of Christ and in the cross as an atonement. We may differ on various dimensions of our understanding of the atonement, but we believe, certainly, that the death of Christ was an atonement. The church still shares one Lord, one faith, and one baptism. If someone is baptized in the Lutheran church and he decides to join the Methodist church, in all probability the Methodist church will recognize the validity of his baptism in the Lutheran church, and from the Methodist to the Anglicans, and so on, because we have one Lord, who is Christ, one faith, and one baptism.

Another important point of unity goes back to the Apostles' Creed. When the Apostles' Creed talks about the church, it talks about the *communion of saints*. I once received a letter from a twenty-six-year-old man who suffered from a terminal illness. He knew he would soon die, and he wrote me to say that he had read my book *Surprised by Suffering*. But he also wanted to tell me that he was ready

(Living Will)

to go home. He was looking forward to spending eternity with Christ. He wrote, "I want you to know I'm going to die in faith." It gave me chills to read this young man's letter. I thought, "If I get the opportunity to speak with this man, I'm going to talk to him about meeting Luther and Augustine and John Calvin and Jonathan Edwards and all the great saints of the past." I would say: "Do you realize that you're about to embark on an adventure that every Christian from the past has already experienced? Every one of them made the pilgrimage through death's door. Everyone who is in Christ died in faith and joined that whole host of witnesses." The fellowship, the mystical communion, that we enjoy as members of the body of Christ transcends the local congregation of which we are a part.

As Christians, when we are worshiping Christ on Sunday morning, we are enjoying fellowship with Christ, and by the Spirit, we are communing with Jesus. As we visit our churches on Sunday morning, though they are part of different denominations and in different towns, we also are enjoying fellowship with Christ. Since Christ is able to be present at your church and at mine, and I am linked to Him and you are linked to Him, we have communion together. The word *communion* is almost a redundancy.

The Latin *unio* means "oneness." And the prefix *com-* simply means "with." So, in the fellowship of the church we are "with union" with other people, and that is part of the oneness of the church. That communion is not only a communion of saints living, but we who are united to Christ in this world are, at least in a mystical sense, communing with those who have gone before us, who are alive and present and abiding in Christ.

The Church Is Holy

In recent years, there have been so many scandals involving religious figures that some people have said, "If there's any institution that is not holy, it's the church." It is often said that the church is full of hypocrites. So we might expect the church fathers, in describing the church, to call it the one, *unholy*, catholic, and Apostolic church.

But no, the fathers called it *holy*. The simple reason is because the Word of God calls it holy. Believers in the New Testament are called the *hagioi*, or the "saints," which means "the holy ones." How can we be called "holy ones" when we are so manifestly unholy? Paul tells the saints who are at Corinth, "Stop all this fighting and this immorality."

Yet he still calls them saints. It seems like a contradiction for sinners to be called holy.

There are several reasons why the church is called holy. The first is because the church, you recall, is *ekklēsia*—called out from the world. Because God has separated this institution from every other human institution, He has consecrated it, and by consecrating it or setting it apart, God has made it holy. The second reason why we call the church holy is because the church members who are truly Christians are indwelt by the Holy Spirit. In other words, the Holy Spirit descends on the church, on the people of God, and makes His dwelling place in them. That doesn't mean that the indwelling of the Holy Spirit automatically conveys or confers perfection. We are not glorified; we are not yet perfectly sanctified. But insofar as the Holy Spirit dwells in us, we are the *hagioi*, the holy ones.

When considering the three persons of the Godhead, I've often wondered why only one of the three is given the title *holy* as part of His name. We know that God is holy, but we don't speak of the Holy Father, and we know that the Son is holy, but we don't talk about the Holy Son. Rather, we speak of Father, Son, and Holy Spirit. Why? Because the emphasis in the ministry of the Holy Spirit as the third member of the Trinity is on making the people of God holy. And so the Spirit, as He works in the institution of the church, is working by the means of grace to sanctify us.

The Church Is Catholic

The third descriptive adjective that the Nicene Creed uses to describe the church is *catholic*. The word *catholic* simply means "universal." In the fourth century, when the Nicene Creed was written, the church of Christ was more clearly universal in the sense that wherever the Christian church was found, whether it was in Greece or in Italy or in England, it was the same "denomination," if you will. It was the same visible institution with the same structure and the same hierarchy, so the church could say, "Where the bishop is, there is the church." Today, given the reality of church splits and the proliferation of denominations, that catholicity in the visible, institutional sense has been lost.

In the sixteenth century, part of the controversy between Rome and the Reformers was over precisely this point. What was Rome to do with the churches that had broken away from Roman Catholic communion, such as the Lutheran church in Germany and the Reformed church in Switzerland and Scotland? Rome said the churches that were springing up in these nations were not true churches because they were not catholic—they were restricted to one nation or to one locality, whereas the Roman church is an international church. The Roman Catholic Church has representatives all over the world. This was one of the arguments that the Roman church in the sixteenth century used against the Protestants: "You are local; we are catholic." But the Protestants said: "The faith that we embrace—the one Lord, one faith, one baptism—is catholic. That remains universal, and we still hold to the catholic faith—the universal doctrine of Christ and of the Scripture—and that catholicity is still an important element of every church."

The various denominations—Presbyterian, Lutheran, Dutch Reformed, Baptist, Methodist, and so on—have certain distinctives, points on which they disagree. But insofar as they hold to the one true faith, they are part of the one catholic church. Anyone who is truly Reformed is part of the one catholic church, likewise anyone who is truly Lutheran. Denominations may obscure the catholicity of the church, in that we do not observe institutional unity, but they do not destroy it. We don't discard our catholicity—the true universal truth of Christianity—when we embrace a particular denomination with its distinctives. All true believers, in every denomination, are part of the one catholic church.

The Church Is Apostolic

Finally, the church is *Apostolic*. I doubt if there has been any time in the history of Christianity where the integrity of the Apostles has come more sharply under attack from within the church than in our own generation. When people attack the authority of the Bible, they are attacking the authority of the Apostles. The early church father Irenaeus had to combat the Gnostics and other groups that said: "We are not going to follow the teachings of the Apostles anymore. We have our own insight; we have our own knowledge; we have our own source of authority. We believe in Jesus, but we are not going to accept the authority of the Apostles." They essentially said, "Jesus we like, but it's Paul we can't stand." But Irenaeus said that if you reject the Apostle Paul, then you reject the One who sent the Apostle, Jesus.

The word *Apostle* simply means "one who is sent." To be an Apostle in the sense in which the New Testament uses the term is not only to be sent by someone but also to be authorized to speak with the authority of the one who sent you. When Irenaeus argued against the heretics, he was merely echoing Jesus' own argument with the Pharisees. The Pharisees said: "We are the children of God. We believe God. It's You, Jesus, that we're not going to accept." How did Jesus handle that? He said, "This is the work of God, that you believe in him whom he has sent" (John 6:29). Jesus was the first Apostle. He was the One whom the Father sent, and the Father sent Him with all authority on heaven and earth (see Matt. 28:18). What Jesus says, the Father says. One of the things that Jesus said when He commissioned the Apostles was, "Whoever receives you receives me, and whoever receives me receives him who sent me" (Matt. 10:40).

We can't have Jesus without Paul. We don't know anything about Jesus except what we have learned through the testimony of the Apostles. Jesus Himself said (and Paul agreed) that the very foundation of the church is the Apostles (see Matt. 16:18; Eph. 2:20).

Some churches believe in an unbroken succession of the Apostolate from the original Twelve down to the present day. In the Roman Catholic Church, the pope is considered the vicar, or priest, of Christ. He is the successor of Peter, who Rome believes was the first bishop of Rome. They believe that a church is not authentically Apostolic unless there is this line of succession from the first century down to today. Protestant churches of the sixteenth century rejected this view of Apostolic succession, stating that Apostolicity comes not from a line of successors but from a line of doctrine. Through the passing down of the true faith, the authority of the Apostles remains intact in the life of the church. Thus, the authority of the Apostles is expressed in the life of the church today through the sacred Scriptures.

Chapter Four

Visible
and Invisible

Many people, when they think of the church, think only of an institution—a group with a building, leaders, members, organization, and so on. But historically, theologians have distinguished between two aspects of the church: the visible church and the invisible church. Augustine of Hippo provided the first in-depth theological exposition of the distinction between the visible and the invisible church, and this distinction is still subject to much misunderstanding and confusion. In this chapter, I want to take us back to the fourth century and try to gain a deeper understanding of that distinction.

In 1960s America, we saw the advent of the so-called underground church. People involved in that movement expressed a disdain for the visible, organized church, and they saw themselves as a conscious alternative to the visible church. By virtue of their loose organization, many considered themselves to be the invisible church—that is, they did not have a visible structure. That reflects a serious misunderstanding of what Augustine had in mind when he distinguished between the visible church and the invisible church. You cannot have one circle or sphere that is called the visible church and then, outside of it, another group of people that is called the invisible church.

For Augustine, the invisible church is found within the visible church. There may be the occasional individual who is part of the invisible church but not part of the visible church, but that would be unusual. Augustine would include in that category people like the thief on the cross, who was converted in his hour of death. He had no opportunity to align himself with a visible institution; there was no opportunity for church membership or even for baptism as he hung on the cross. We know that at certain times in history, at points of crisis, people are dragged away from society and thrown into prison or into some kind of isolated situation where they have no opportunity to align themselves with a body of other Christians. Those people who are truly members of the body of Christ because of their faith remain, at least for a season, outside the visible church.

There is one other possibility by which a person could be in the invisible church and not be in the visible church. A person could truly be a child of God but because of spiritual immaturity might have a seriously defective view of the church. Maybe he has been disappointed in his local congregation, and he has not yet been exposed to the teaching of Scripture. He might be a new convert and think, "I don't want to make the mistake of falling into the trap of institutionalism." But we would assume that once that person understood the teaching of the New Testament, if he were indeed regenerate of the Holy Spirit, he would hear the voice of his Lord commanding him to be a part of His body, and his disobedience would end at that point.

There is also the opposite situation. Some people have their names on the rolls of the visible church, but they are not children of God. They are unbelievers, and they are outside the kingdom of God. They're part of the visible church community, but they are not part of the invisible church, which is made up only of the elect, those who have been called by the work of the Holy Spirit and brought to true faith.

Augustine spoke to this situation as well. He said that the church is a body, a *corpus*, but it is a *corpus per mixtum*—a mixed body. Augustine drew this conclusion from the teachings of Jesus. Jesus says the church includes tares or weeds that live and grow among the wheat (Matt. 13:24–30); that is, the visible church includes unbelievers as well as believers. This calls for caution in the administration of church discipline. According to the process of church discipline that Christ instituted, an unrepentant individual who is engaged in gross and heinous sin is finally expelled from the body and assumed to be an unbeliever (Matt. 18:15–20). However, Christ placed constraints on how church discipline is exercised, and the church is to take great care not to hastily excommunicate someone, out of the concern not to wrongfully expel from the church someone who is truly a child of God. So, though Jesus instituted excommunication, He fenced that process with great care and caution. It is better that the church continue living with weeds growing up within it than that, in its zeal to purify the church, it ruthlessly rip up the wheat that God has planted and destroy it along with the tares.

Jesus also uses the image of the sheep and the goats (Matt. 25:31–46). The sheep are those who truly belong to Christ, who truly love Him and embrace Him; the goats are those whose confession of faith is spurious or false. Jesus indicated that it is possible for people to make a profession of faith and do all the things that are required by the visible church to enter into membership. A person can go through a membership class, give a credible profession of faith, receive the sign of baptism, and do all of those things that are required for church membership. He may even be a scrupulous tither, be involved in the life of the church, attend the services regularly and punctually—all this while holding to a false profession of faith. Jesus said of such false converts, "This people honors me with their lips, but their heart is far from me" (Matt. 15:8).

Of course, the claims of the mouth are things we can perceive outwardly. They belong to the visible (or the audible) realm. But the reason Augustine calls the inner core of true believers the "invisible church" is because the thing that is invisible about them is their hearts. The Bible says man looks on the outward appearances, but God looks on the heart (1 Sam. 16:7). The invisible church, therefore, is invisible to us. But it's not invisible to God. Christ knows His sheep (John 10:14). He knows who are authentically His; He can read their hearts just as He read the thoughts of the woman of Samaria (John 4). God can read the state of our souls without seeing any external visible evidence of our faith. He knows who is truly redeemed and who isn't— but we don't. We can be fooled. People can make a good outward appearance of godliness. We call that the problem of hypocrisy.

After I first became a Christian, I had a discussion with a friend who prided himself on his academic skepticism. He was contemptuous of the truth claims of Christianity. As I spoke to him about my newfound faith, he exhibited disdain for my naivete and mocked me for my convictions. I remember how troubled in spirit I was. The next morning, I went to church, and I looked across the aisle, and there was my friend sitting with his parents. I noticed that when it came time to say the Apostles' Creed, he stood just like everyone else, and he said, "I believe in God, the Father Almighty." He said it for anyone who was present to hear him; he gave an outward profession of faith. He honored God with his lips, while the night before he had shown how far his heart was from God when he expressed his utter contempt for the Christian faith.

The day I was examined by my presbytery for ordination, one of my friends who was also going to be examined asked me, "Should I go with the resurrection of Christ or not?" I asked, "What do you mean?" He said, "Well, should I say that I believe in the resurrection of Christ?" I queried, "Well, do you?" He responded: "I haven't believed that in years. How can anyone be acquainted with our critical theories and still embrace the resurrection of Christ? But I know that some of those people out there are going to insist that I say that." He went on to stand before the presbytery, and he perjured himself by declaring that he believed something that he didn't believe.

In church history there are times that God so renews His church and the church experiences awakening to spiritual things that the visible church is composed almost completely of those who are truly in the faith. But there are also dark moments in church history where the church falls into deep corruption and disobedience so that churches become, as the Scriptures suggest, synagogues of Satan, where we are fortunate to find just a fragment of the invisible church in the visible church. Remember what happened in the Old Testament: the whole nation of Israel was called into fellowship with God and the whole nation participated externally in the visible church of Israel, in the covenant community. But by the time the Old Testament was drawing to a close, the hope for the future was that a tiny remnant would still be faithful.

There is another danger. Sometimes we're so acutely conscious of the problem of the visible and the invisible church that we reduce the possible number of those in the invisible church down to a dot. We suffer from what I call the Elijah syndrome. Do you remember when Elijah complained to God that he was trying to be faithful in the midst of a people who were collectively unfaithful? Priests and prophets together were going in a completely different direction from Elijah, and finally he lamented, "I, even I only, am left" (1 Kings 19:14). God had to rebuke him, saying that He preserves His people: "I will leave seven thousand in Israel, all the knees that have not bowed to Baal, and every mouth that has not kissed him" (v. 18). From Elijah's perspective, everywhere he looked, he saw people on their knees before Baal; he couldn't find seven, not to mention seven thousand, worshipers of the true God. But God knew who His people were.

Again, the point of the distinction between the visible and the invisible has to do with the state of the soul. One of the most terrifying warnings Jesus gives comes in His conclusion to the Sermon on the Mount:

> Not everyone who says to me, "Lord, Lord," will enter the kingdom of heaven, but the one who does the will of my Father who is in heaven. On that day many will say to me, "Lord, Lord, did we not prophesy in your name, and cast out demons in your name, and do many mighty works in your name?" And then will I declare to them, "I never knew you; depart from me, you workers of lawlessness." (Matt. 7:21–23)

The repetition of the form of address—"Lord, Lord"— indicates a personal, intimate relationship. These people believe that they have a deep, personal relationship with Jesus. But what scares me is that not just some but *many* actually believe they have a personal relationship with Christ. To this multitude, Jesus will say on the last day, "Please leave Me; I don't know your name." They're going to protest: "But Lord, I was a preacher"; "I prophesied"; "I did miracles"; "I cast demons out of people"; "Look at the track record of the wonderful works I performed in the name of the church." Jesus will say to these workers of lawlessness, "Please leave." Again, they are people who say they love Christ but refuse to keep His commandments.

John Calvin struggled with the distinction between the visible church and the invisible church because, while the hearts of the faithful are known only to God, it is not as if the invisible church is to have an invisible presence. Rather, Calvin said, the task of the invisible church is to make itself visible. Those who have true faith are to be a light to the world, to make their faith manifest, that we may bear witness to the Lord whose church we are.

Chapter Five

When to Leave a Church

We've already seen that it is possible for an individual to make a spurious or counterfeit profession of faith. Is it possible for a whole collection of individuals who make up the corporate visible church to have a false profession? Or can a church become so corrupt that it ceases, in any real sense of the term, to be a church? In other words, when is the church not the church? The answer to that question affects our decisions to join or to leave particular church bodies, and answering it depends on how we understand the nature of the church.

To understand what a true church is, it is helpful to consider when the church began. There are a few different answers to this question that are based on various aspects of the church and that help us understand what the church is.

In his essay *"Ecclesia ab Abel,"* the French Roman Catholic theologian Yves Congar traces the roots of the church back to Abel. He contrasts Abel's act of worship before God (his sacrifice) with Cain's counterfeit sacrifice that was apparently offered insincerely. Abel's act of worship was delightful and acceptable to God, whereas Cain's was not, and in his fury, Cain rose up and slew his brother. Congar wants to go all the way back to Abel to find the beginning of the church in terms of acceptable worship.

We could even go back further. We could say that the church began in Eden, for wherever there is fellowship between God and His creatures, there is the church, and man was created to worship God. Before the fall, when God walked with Adam and Eve in the cool of the evening, surely they prostrated themselves before Him in adoration, service, and worship. So, we could say, in one sense, the church began in Eden.

But if we understand the church as the elect, as Augustine did, we would push it back even further. We could say that the church began at the foundation of the world when God chose individuals in Christ for salvation (Eph. 1:3–6).

Taking another approach, if we look only at New Testament history when considering the origins of the church, many different moments come to mind, including the day of Christ's crucifixion, Easter, and Pentecost. Another is the Last Supper in the upper room, where Jesus celebrated the Passover with His disciples one last time. Jesus made intricate provisions for them to meet around the table and to celebrate Passover. The Passover liturgy followed the pattern God established in the book of Exodus, each element symbolizing an act of God's redemption. As they went through this meal and recited the liturgy, Jesus suddenly deviated from the script and changed the program. He took the bread and said, "This is my body" (Matt. 26:26). That wasn't in the old covenant liturgy of the Passover. Then He took the cup of wine and said, "This is my blood of the covenant" (v. 28), thereby announcing the inauguration of the new covenant Jeremiah had promised centuries before (Jer. 31:31–34). The covenant that Jesus announced in the upper room was ratified the next afternoon, when Christ poured out His blood for His church.

Another moment that some have chosen as the beginning of the church is the death of Stephen (Acts 7), because Stephen's death provoked a crisis in the nascent Christian community. The original Christian church was made up almost exclusively of converts from Judaism. But the conflict between the Jewish authorities and the emerging Christian community became so severe that in a short period of time, Christian views were no longer tolerable to the visible household of Israel. When Stephen was killed for his testimony to Christ, this marked a serious rupture between the Jewish community and the emerging Christian community.

But it didn't destroy the fellowship between Jews and Christians altogether. After Stephen's death and the subsequent persecution of Christians in Jerusalem (Acts 8:1–3), Saul, who had held the coats of those who stoned Stephen, later preached the good news of Christ in synagogues. In other words, until at least AD 70, there was a pattern whereby the persecuted minority of Christians tried to maintain a relationship with the Jewish community even in the midst of being persecuted.

This point is important. We're living in a day of unprecedented church splits where people seem to be willing to leave a church or divide a church over trivial matters—not crucial doctrines like the Trinity, but things like personality conflicts and disputes over minor points. Division within the visible church community is clearly not always called for—but it is sometimes necessary. There are, in fact, times when a church becomes so corrupt that not only *may* one depart from its midst but one *must* leave it. This applies both to church splits, when a group leaves a church body and forms a new church body or joins another body, and to individuals, when a person or family decides to leave a particular congregation. When do such radical crises occur?

Before we answer that, let's go back to the sixteenth century. This was a time when Christians had to really wrestle with that question. When Luther nailed the Ninety-Five Theses to the church door in Wittenberg, Germany, he had no idea what the ramifications of his actions would be. It was common for university scholars at that time to call for academic and theological discussions, and Luther wanted to have a discussion about indulgence sales in Germany. His Ninety-Five Theses were meant to spark a debate. Soon, however, his theses were duplicated many times over (thanks to the recent invention of the printing press), and copies were being carried all across Germany. The Protestant Reformation was off and running.

Luther had no idea that his actions would help bring about one of the deepest divisions in the history of Christendom. When he went through the painful experience of being censored for his doctrine of justification by faith alone, another crisis occurred. Pope Leo X issued a papal bull that excommunicated Luther, the opening words of which were: "Rise up, O Lord. There's a wild boar loose in Your vineyard." That wild boar, according to the pope, was Martin Luther. The pope condemned Luther and sent him outside the visible church.

But Luther didn't remain silent, and as he was excommunicated, thousands joined him and the other Reformers. John Calvin was originally interested in becoming a priest in the Roman Catholic Church, but as a matter of conscience, he aligned himself with the teaching of Luther. New churches began departing from the old. People asked, "Is this justifiable, to go so far as to break communion and fellowship with the church that has existed for hundreds of years?"

In *The Bondage of the Will*, Luther responded to the Roman Catholic scholar Desiderius Erasmus. Luther thanked

Erasmus for not troubling him over trivial matters. But they dueled on issues Luther considered supremely important to the people of God. For example, echoing Augustine, Luther called the doctrine of election the *cor ecclesia*, the heart of the church. He considered the doctrine of justification by faith alone, which was the material issue of the sixteenth-century Reformation, the article upon which the church stands or falls. Now, one may not agree with Luther's assessment, but Luther was convinced that justification by faith alone is supremely important because it touches on the question of how a person is redeemed, and that has eternal consequences.

This wasn't a question of what color to paint the church basement. This was a real conflict, and Luther said he was willing to stand up against every authority structure in the world because of the importance of the issue. Luther believed that if he didn't defy the church authorities, he would be acting in defiance to God. So, the choice, in Luther's mind, was either treason to Christ or treason to the church.

That is a horrible choice for any person to have to make. But to some degree or another, many of us will face that same dilemma, because we are living in a time when the visible church in some places makes the sixteenth-century

Roman Catholic Church look almost pure by contrast. Not only is justification by faith denied in some circles, but the deity of Christ is denied. Some churches even deny the very existence of God. All sorts of heinous sins are not only tolerated but also endorsed among some churches in our age.

Is this simply a temporary fall from grace, from which those in question might return, or are we witnessing apostasy? Apostasy is what happened in Israel, when the false prophets denied their first profession of faith. An apostate is one who, having first made a profession of faith, later repudiates it. It's a dreadful word to ascribe to anyone, but to use it to describe a church is radical indeed. In the sixteenth century, the Reformers had to ask whether the visible church centered on Rome had descended into apostasy.

The climate of conflict is far different today than it was in the sixteenth century. But the Reformation was a necessary time of theological reflection among Protestants. It forced them to ask, What are the marks of a true church? Answering that question allowed them to determine whether they could remain in fellowship with Rome or whether they would be forced to break away. They determined that there are three marks of a true church, and understanding and applying these marks in our own contexts can allow us to think through whether to leave a particular church.

The first mark, the Reformers determined, was that the gospel is preached. A true church preaches the gospel.

The second mark is the administration of the sacraments. The Roman Catholic Church has seven sacraments, but the Protestant movement reduced that number to two—baptism and the Lord's Supper. Some tried to eliminate the sacraments altogether, but the Reformers said that if you take away the sacraments, you take away the church. So, according to the Reformers, any professing Christian body that denies the sacraments no longer has the right to claim to be a true church.

The third mark is discipline. In the past, the church used torturous methods of discipline, like subjecting people to the rack and burning people at the stake. They believed that any kind of corporal punishment was justified if it could redeem a person from the torment of eternal hell. As misguided as such practices were, the church authorities believed they were doing the right thing. Today, following the Reformers, discipline does not consist of bodily punishments but is restricted to spiritual censures, including admonition, suspension from the sacraments, and excom-munication. It is designed to reclaim the wayward, safeguard the purity of the church, and protect the honor of Christ's name.

But the central issue is the first mark: Is the gospel preached? Related to this is another question: How pure must the gospel that is preached be for a church to be a true church? We know some people will split off and start a new church over the tiniest point of doctrinal dis-pute. For some, any disagreement is grounds to separate from a church and start their own church. This was not the view of the Reformers. When they said that the gos-pel is preached, they meant that the gospel is preached *essentially*. That is, the essence of the gospel is held by the church and is proclaimed by the church. What is the essence? It's the necessary ingredients without which it wouldn't be the gospel. For example, if a church denies the atonement of Christ, it denies the gospel, because the atonement of Jesus is essential to the biblical doctrine of salvation.

Every error we embrace—and we all embrace many of them—affects the well-being of the gospel and therefore affects the well-being of the church. But not every error is so serious that it involves denying or rejecting something that is essential to the gospel. So, the Reformers asserted that when an institution denies or rejects something that is essential to the gospel, then that church ceases to be a church. That's why Protestants and the Roman Catholic Church do not recognize Mormons or Jehovah's Witnesses as fellow members of the household of faith. Those organizations deny the deity of Christ, and the historic Christian church has held that the deity of Christ is of the essence of Christianity. Likewise, Luther said that justification by faith alone is of the essence of the gospel, and any church body that repudiates it is not a valid church.

The first mark of the church is perhaps the most important, and to fail on that point is for a body to invalidate itself as a true church. The same goes for the other two marks. If the sacraments are rejected or blasphemed or if the discipline of the church reaches such a level that the church openly and actively endorses gross and heinous sin, then, according to the Reformers, the institution in question is no longer a true church.

In applying these marks as individuals and families, we must be careful and patient. Church bodies, like individuals, are capable of serious falls, yet they still can be restored if they repent. We have to be careful not to err in one of two directions: on the one hand, we must not be too hasty to separate; on the other hand, we must be careful not to tolerate the intolerable and in so doing identify with the denial of Christ.

Chapter Six

To the Ends
of the Earth

What is the mission of the church in the world? This is an important question that bears on our responsibility as members of the church in this age.

When I was a seminary student preparing for the ministry, I had the opportunity to spend time with an elderly minister. After I had quizzed him on a number of things, he turned the tables and asked me a somewhat provocative question. "R.C.," he said, "is the church more like an army, or is it more like a hospital?" I didn't hesitate for a second.

I knew the answer to that question cold. I said: "That's simple. The church is an army." I was fired up. I was a young man, I had enlisted in the battle, I had enrolled for the duration, and I saw the primary task of the church as that of a spiritual army fighting for the kingdom of God. I didn't view the church principally as a place where people could go to have their wounds tended. That's typical of youth, who get more excited about adventure, battle, and conquest than about ministry to those who are in pain, who are lonely, or who are hurting. Of course, this wise minister lovingly rebuked me and told me that the question was intentionally a false dilemma. He said, "Son, the church is both an army and a hospital."

It is sometimes said that the church is the only army that shoots its own wounded. This cynical statement probably reflects people's experiences of not having felt properly ministered to by the church. Now, we do go to the church to be ministered to. But as we experience the healing that the church has to offer, we also enter the warfare that, as the Apostle Paul says, is not against flesh and blood but against powers and principalities and spiritual wickedness in the high places (Eph. 6:12). For the church to be the church, it must, in this world, be the church militant—it is engaged in battle. It is not yet the church triumphant—the church that has conquered and is glorified. No one can be victorious in the battle without first being in the battle. Scripture clearly calls us to a battle.

Consider the martyrdom of Stephen, which was a watershed moment in church history. The Jewish authorities condemned him as a heretic, when in fact he was proclaiming the true faith. After the record of his death in Acts 7, we read these words:

> And Saul approved of his execution. And there arose on that day a great persecution against the church in Jerusalem, and they were all scattered throughout the regions of Judea and Samaria, except the apostles. Devout men buried Stephen and made great lamentation over him. But Saul was ravaging the church, and entering house after house, he dragged off men and women and committed them to prison. Now those who were scattered went about preaching the word. (8:1–4)

Acts 8 records an important point of transition in the early church. We're told at the beginning of the chapter that a great persecution arose against the church in Jerusalem. Why was the church in Jerusalem in the first place? Remember that when Jesus ascended, He told His disciples to wait in Jerusalem (1:4). He said, "You will receive power when the Holy Spirit has come upon you" (v. 8), and He instructed them to wait for that power from on high. What was the purpose of that power? Christ was going to pour out His Spirit on His church to empower them for the mission that they had been given, and He also set forth the purpose of that task. At Christ's ascension, the last question the disciples asked was, "Lord, will you at this time restore the kingdom to Israel?" (v. 6). Jesus virtually ignored that question and said, "You will be my witnesses in Jerusalem and in all Judea and Samaria, and to the end of the earth" (v. 8).

The commission Christ gave the church began in Jerusalem and then moved outward to Judea and then to Samaria and then to the whole earth. The context for that commission was the disciples' question regarding the character of the kingdom of God ("Will you at this time restore the kingdom to Israel?"). Jesus essentially said: "You are mistaken in your question. It is not for you to know times or seasons." Jesus was ascending to His Father in heaven, to His coronation, and to His investiture as the King of the kings and as the Lord of the lords, but His kingdom is invisible.

Recall that Pilate was looking for Jesus' kingdom at His trial: "Are you the King of the Jews?" (John 18:33). Jesus said, "My kingdom is not of this world" (v. 36). Does that mean that He has no dominion over this world, that the sphere of His authority doesn't include this world? Not at all; on the contrary, all authority in heaven and earth has been given to Christ. At the ascension, He was enthroned, so the King of kings is already seated in the place of cosmic authority.

Do you think that the power brokers in Washington, D.C., consult with the King of kings every day before they make decisions? Do you think the politicians in the world are concerned with carrying out the will of the One who is the King over them? No, at this time no one can see Christ in His exalted state of cosmic authority. The kingdom of God right now is invisible.

What is the primary task that Christ gives to the church? Remember that the chief function of the church, as Calvin said, is to make the invisible church visible. That is, every Christian is called be a witness. In Christian jargon, we tend to use the term *witnessing* as a synonym for *evangelism*, but they are not synonyms in the Bible. The generic term is *witnessing*. One of the sub-meanings of *witnessing* is "evangelism." We tend to reverse that in our Christian speech. In other words, there are all kinds of ways by which the church is called to bear witness to the kingdom of God and to the lordship of Christ. One of the most important is clearly the preaching of the gospel, the work of evangelism. That's a vital form of witness, but when the church ministers to the poor, feeds the hungry, gives water to the thirsty and clothes to the naked, or visits prisoners in jail, then the church is making visible the reign of Christ.

Our general task is to bear witness, whether by ministry to the sick or to the imprisoned, by having integrity in our jobs, or by verbally preaching the gospel. Those are all forms of witness. Interestingly, the Greek word that we translate as "witness" is *marturia*; this is also where we get our word *martyr*. Those who have borne witness to the kingdom of God even to death are called martyrs—not because they died, but because they bore witness, making the invisible kingdom of God visible through their profession of faith and through their obedience. But martyrdom occurs only when the church is the church militant. The world isn't interested in killing deserters from an army that has surrendered. It is only when we take our faith seriously as Christians that we risk martyrdom.

The church of the first century didn't have to wait long before persecution descended on it. Jesus had warned them: "If the world has hated Me, they're going to hate you. You're going to have to take up your cross. When you identify with Me, you must be willing to participate in My humiliation and disgrace and in My suffering if you ever want to participate in My glory and in My exaltation." He had hardly left when the fire of persecution fell on the early church and caused such severe travail that the Christian community had to flee Jerusalem.

In the providence of God, it was persecution that drove the church out of Jerusalem and into Judea and Samaria and into the uttermost parts of the earth. Acts 8:4 reads, "Now those who were scattered went about preaching the word." That was the net effect of persecution. Where the church was persecuted, it was scattered, but wherever it was scattered, those who were scattered went everywhere preaching the Word.

Who were those who were scattered? "And they were all scattered throughout the regions of Judea and Samaria, except the apostles" (v. 1). The church militant of the first century was a church with a mobilized laity. The Apostles stayed in Jerusalem. It was the laypeople who scattered and did the work of evangelism.

One of the primary tasks of the church is to equip the saints for ministry. The church is here not only to nurture our souls and prepare us for heaven but also to train us and assist us in gaining the skills to minister in this world. Every Christian is called to participate in the ministry of the church in some way, and it's only when the laity becomes mobilized that the church militant makes an impact on the world. That's why Ligonier Ministries is dedicated to helping laypeople become equipped, knowledgeable, and articulate. We need trained and skilled people who enlist in the army of Christ.

It is more normal than abnormal in the history of Christianity to be persecuted. When we're not persecuted, it's not because we've already won the battle and now everyone's a Christian. The reason we're not persecuted is because we're not considered a threat to anyone. We have been assigned to a reservation, and the government has said: "As long as you behave yourself and live within the confines of the reservation, you have all the freedom and protection to pray as much as you want, to read the Bible as much as you want, and to sing all the hymns you want. But if you dare step off that reservation, it will cost you your head. Don't come into the public arena with your faith." When we try that, we see how soon the hammer of persecution falls. But the early church was fighting for the kingdom of God, and they were prepared to be casualties for Christ.

In the roll call of faith found in Hebrews 11, the author concludes his rehearsal of the great deeds of faith of the heroes of the past by saying: "What more shall I say? For time would fail me to tell of Gideon, Barak, Samson, Jephthah, of David and Samuel and the prophets—who through faith conquered kingdoms, enforced justice, obtained promises, [and] stopped the mouths of lions" (Heb. 11:32–33). That's the church militant. They "quenched the power of fire, escaped the edge of the sword, were made strong out of weakness, became mighty in war, put foreign armies to flight. Women received back their dead by resurrection. Some were tortured, refusing to accept release, so that they might rise again to a better life. Others suffered mocking and flogging, and even chains and imprisonment. They were stoned, they were sawn in two, they were killed with the sword. They went about in skins of sheep and goats, destitute, afflicted, mistreated—of whom the world was not worthy" (vv. 34–38). All of them were looking for a better city, whose builder and maker is God (v. 10). Each of them, at the end of his or her pilgrimage, passed over the line from the church militant and entered the church triumphant. Unless we're willing to fight and to die, we are not being faithful to the mission of the church.

Even if we are not persecuted to the point for death for our witness, we are called to join the church in its mission. The church, the body of Christ, has a task to do, and as members of that body, we are called to join in that task. The church cannot fulfill its mission without us, and we cannot do what we are called to do on our own. We need the church, and the church needs us.

About the Author

Dr. R.C. Sproul was founder of Ligonier Ministries, founding pastor of Saint Andrew's Chapel in Sanford, Fla., first president of Reformation Bible College, and executive editor of *Tabletalk* magazine. His radio program, *Renewing Your Mind*, is still broadcast daily on hundreds of radio stations around the world and can also be heard online. He was author of more than one hundred books, including *The Holiness of God*, *Chosen by God*, and *Everyone's a Theologian*. He was recognized throughout the world for his articulate defense of the inerrancy of Scripture and the need for God's people to stand with conviction upon His Word.

Get 3 free months
of *Tabletalk*

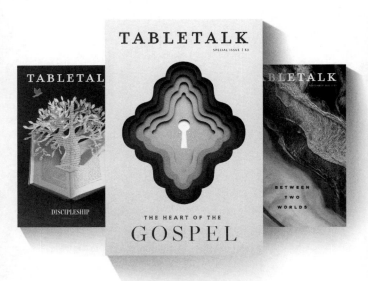

In 1977, R.C. Sproul started *Tabletalk* magazine.
Today it has become the most widely read subscriber-based monthly
devotional magazine in the world. **Try it free for 3 months.**

TryTabletalk.com/CQ | 800.435.4343